Let's Cook Together

With 40 Fun, Healthy Recipes

DK | Penguin Random House

Senior Editor Tori Kosara
Senior Art Editor Lauren Adams
Production Editor Marc Staples
Senior Production Controller Lloyd Robertson
Managing Editor Paula Regan
Managing Art Editor Jo Connor
Managing Director Mark Searle

Edited and designed for DK by XAB Design
www.xabdesign.com

Art Director Nigel Wright
Designers Nigel Wright, Jan Browne
Managing Editor Katie Hardwicke
Photography Nigel Wright
Food Stylist Ellie Jarvis
Prop Stylist Jan Browne

First published in Great Britain in 2024 by
Dorling Kindersley Limited
DK, One Embassy Gardens, 8 Viaduct Gardens,
London, SW11 7BW

The authorised representative in the EEA is
Dorling Kindersley Verlag GmbH. Arnulfstr. 124,
80636 Munich, Germany

Page design copyright © 2024 Dorling Kindersley Limited
A Penguin Random House Company
10 9 8 7 6 5 4 3 2 1
001–339776–July/2024

A CIP catalogue record for this book
is available from the British Library.
ISBN: 978-0-2416-6225-0

Printed and bound in China

www.dk.com
www.sesamestreet.org

MIX
Paper | Supporting
responsible forestry
FSC™ C018179

This book was made with Forest
Stewardship Council™ certified
paper – one small step in DK's
commitment to a sustainable future.
Learn more at www.dk.com/uk/
information/sustainability

Safety disclaimer

All the activities in this book require adult supervision. Always ensure that adults and children follow instructions carefully. The Publisher has made every effort to set out basic safety guidelines as needed. However, it is the responsibility of every user of this book to assess any individual circumstances and potential dangers of any activity they wish to undertake. The Publisher cannot accept any liability for injury, loss, or damage to any user or property following the suggestions in this book.

The Publisher would like to draw the reader's attention to the following particular points:

- Always ensure that children are supervised when engaging in any of the activities suggested in this book, and always take care when using appliances, hot pans, and sharp objects.
- Always thoroughly wash hands before and after handling raw meat or raw eggs.
- Some of the materials suggested by the author can cause damage, such as staining. Always take appropriate precautions to avoid damage to personal items, including clothing and furniture.
- The recipes contained in this book have been created for the ingredients and techniques indicated. The Publisher is not responsible for the reader's specific health or allergy needs. Nor is the Publisher responsible for any adverse reactions you may have to the recipes contained in this book, whether you follow them as written or modify them to your personal taste or dietary requirements.

Acknowledgements

Dorling Kindersley would like to thank Gabriela Arenas, David K. Chan, Jessica Dissalvo, Svetlana Keselman, Lili Lampasona, Louis Henry Mitchell, Meg Roth, Susan Scheiner, Lisa Terzo, and Rosemarie Truglio, Ph.D. at Sesame Workshop. Also, thanks to former Sesame Workshop art director Peter MacKennan and Sesame Workshop nutritional consultant, Wahida Karmally.

DK also thanks Anne Damerell for her contribution to the book, Stephanie Farrow for proofreading, Helen Peters for compiling the index, Julia March for Anglicizing, and Olivia Campbell for editorial assistance.

Contents

Get Ready to Cook!

Join Elmo and Grover and all their Sesame Street friends, and learn how to cook! This is **your own cookbook** for you to choose delicious meals to make for breakfast, lunch, and dinner, along with tasty snacks and healthy treats.

A cookbook is full of **recipes**. These are instructions on how to cook meals. Recipes show you what **ingredients** you need and how to get everything ready. Then they tell you how to mix it, stir it, beat it, **cook it**, or bake it!

Helping in the kitchen can be a lot of fun! You get to **learn all about food** and taste new things. You can practise **counting** and **measuring** as you weigh out ingredients. You can **decorate your dishes** to make them look amazing, too.

You'll find recipes on the pages that follow that even look like your **favourite characters**! Check out Big Bird Sunshine Dip on page 54 or Elmo Spaghetti on page 96. Who else can you find?

Once you've cooked a **delicious meal** or prepared a healthy snack, you **get to eat it**! Some recipes are great for **sharing with a friend** and some are perfect for sitting down around the table with your **family to enjoy together**.

So, **choose a recipe** with a grown-up, put on your apron, grab a spoon, and start cooking!

Healthy Choices

The recipes in this book use ingredients that are good for your growing body. You will soon know how to **choose the best foods** for staying healthy and happy!

Eat well

Your body needs three meals a day – **breakfast**, **lunch**, and **dinner** – made with different types of anytime foods. These include **whole grains**, low-fat **milk** or **yogurt**, **fruit** and **vegetables**, and fish, meat, or plant-based options. You can add some snacks and even treats, or sometimes foods, all of which can be made with healthy ingredients.

HEALTHY HABITS

Check out the **Healthy Habits tips** to find more ideas for making healthy choices when you are **shopping**, **cooking**, and **eating**.

Food is fuel

The best foods to eat are those that have lots of **nutrients** and **fibre**. These give your body energy to **run, play, dance,** and **exercise.** Start your day with a healthy **breakfast** to fuel all your morning activities and top up with an **energy-packed lunch** or an on-the-go snack.

Healthy swaps

As you **help make these recipes** you will discover which foods you can swap for healthier versions, like **swapping** white pasta for wholemeal pasta or adding some **juicy fruit** to **sweeten your porridge** instead of sugar.

Choose fresh

Fresh fruit and vegetables are full of **vitamins** and **minerals.** These are used by your body to help keep you healthy and **help you grow.** Some foods are called **superfoods,** such as avocados, salmon, tomatoes, blueberries, and spinach. Superfoods have lots of nutrients that keep you **active** and keep your body and brain **healthy.** How many superfood ingredients can you find?

Kitchen Safety

Always cook with a grown-up. They will do the chopping with sharp knives, operate electrical gadgets, such as food processors, and use the hot hob or oven, while you get to help in lots of other ways. Before you start to cook, there are a few things to remember to keep you safe around the kitchen:

- Always wash your hands with soap and water before cooking so that you don't mix in germs.

- Rinse fruit and vegetables in water before you eat or cook with them to get rid of any dirt and germs.

- Tie back long hair, roll up your sleeves, and put on an apron to help keep your clothes clean.

- Sit comfortably at a table or the worktop to help prepare the food.

- Listen carefully to instructions from grown-ups.

- Keep away from a hot hob or oven, and hot pans.

- Do not use anything sharp.

Stay safe

Some people are **allergic** or intolerant to certain foods, which can make them ill. It is important for an adult to **check the ingredients** in a recipe before you cook it so that everyone is able to enjoy the recipe safely.

Helping hand

Cooking together with a grownup is lots of fun. You will **learn lots of skills by watching** as they cook, and you can help out, too. Look for the **Helping hand** tips for ideas.

Getting Started

Cooking is a **skill you can learn**, just like dancing or riding a bike! You will need to **follow instructions** that tell you to cook the food in the right order. Then everything is ready to eat at the same time, **and will taste delicious**.

Some recipes need you to prepare or cook the ingredients in **special ways**. Here are a few skills that you can **practise as you cook**. Ask a **grown-up to show you how** and soon you will be ready to cook and put on a chef's hat, just like Gonger!

• Cracking an egg
Tap the shell firmly on the side of a bowl. Gently pull the shell in half along the crack. Tip the whole egg into the bowl.

• Separating an egg
To separate the yolk (the yellow part) from the white (the clear liquid), crack the egg and pull the shell apart. Then pass the yolk gently **back and forth** from one shell to the other. Let the **egg white** drip into the bowl below. **Put the yolk** in a different bowl. Always wash your hands with **soap and water** after handling raw eggs.

• Folding
This means to use a spoon or spatula to mix ingredients by **lifting and turning** them from the bottom of the bowl to the top.

• Kneading
This means folding the dough **over and over** on the worktop, and pushing it out with your palms. You will need some super strength!

• Beating
This means to quickly stir ingredients **around and around** with a fork or whisk to mix everything together.

• Measuring
Using the **right amount** of each ingredient makes a meal taste just right. You can help with the **important jobs** of weighing, counting, and measuring. **Scoop** dry ingredients, like flour or spices, in measuring spoons. **Count out** how many spoonfuls you need – 1, 2, 3, or more!

Cooking Tools

Help get all the **cooking tools ready** before you cook. This is called **preparation**. Remember, grown-ups are **always in charge** of knives and electrical gadgets, **or using hot pots and pans** on the hob or in the oven.

Here are some cooking tools that you can safely learn to use when you help a grown-up cook.

- **Measuring spoons**
Fill measuring spoons level with the top **to get the right amount** for your recipe.

- **Whisk or fork**
Use this to **beat eggs** for an omelette or mix batter for muffins.

- **Wooden spoon and mixing bowl**
Get ready to **stir**!

Chef's tip

Look out for the Chef's tips in the recipes to find **special ways of cooking** or ideas for **different ingredients**, just like a real chef!

- **Rolling pin**
This is fun to use to roll, **flatten**, and smooth dough for **cookies**, **pizzas**, and other recipes.

- **Sieve or strainer**
These are great for **rinsing fruit or veggies**, or for squashing berries to make a delicious sauce. You can **use your hands** for rinsing ingredients, too.

- **Cookie cutters**
You can use any shape cookie cutter you like. A jar lid or cup also makes a great circle cutter. Number cutters help you **learn to count**, or use alphabet cutters to practise your **ABCs**!

Rolling pin

Sieve

Whisk

Measuring spoons

Cookie cutters

Food is Fun!

Cooking together with a grown-up is a **special time** and a great activity to share with a friend, too. There are **exciting tastes** to discover, new skills to learn, and lots of time for **creative play**!

Find fun ways to use **maths** in the kitchen. You can **count** and measure, or **sort** by size and colour. Look for **shapes** that you can make, such as triangle-shaped pizza slices or circle-shaped apple rings.

Grow your own
Lots of recipes use **herbs to add extra flavour**. Why not grow a kitchen herb garden on your windowsill? Try **basil**, **parsley**, and **coriander**. Which herb is your favourite?

Discover where food comes from. **Visiting a farm** with your family is a big treat, especially if you can pick some of the food yourself, or choose some fruit and veggies from a farm stall or your local supermarket.

Serve in style
Making your **food look good** before you eat it is the final part of cooking a meal. Putting food on the plate is called **serving**. Arrange each piece of food, making sure everyone has the **same amount**, or **portion**. Then add some finishing touches, such as **sprinkles of grated cheese** or **herbs**. Yum!

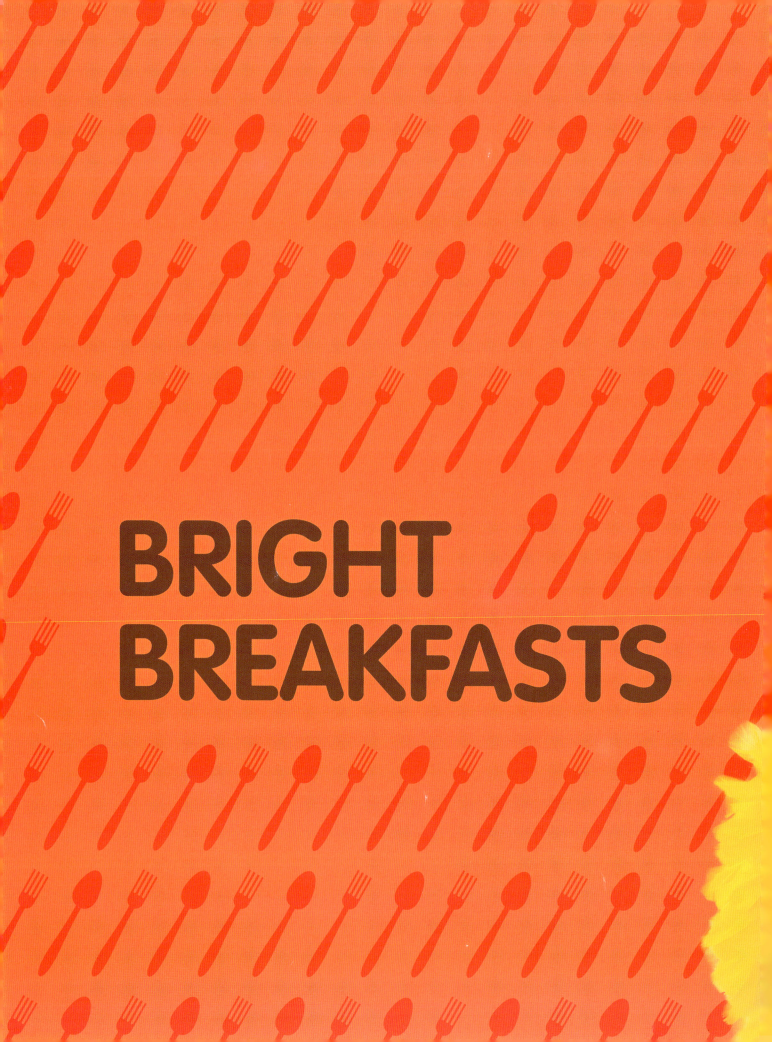

BRIGHT BREAKFASTS

✱✱✱✱✱✱✱✱✱✱✱✱✱✱✱✱✱

Rise and Shine Oats

Wake up, **breakfast is ready**! Soak chewy oats and sweet fruit in milk and yogurt overnight and you can **tuck in straight away** in the morning. Chia seeds will give you **lots of energy for playtime** later.

 SERVES 2

 10 prep plus overnight

Ingredients

- 4 tablespoons low-fat Greek yogurt
- 5 tablespoons low-fat (semi-skimmed) milk
- 50 grams (1¾ ounces) porridge oats
- 2 teaspoons chia seeds
- ½ small peach, peeled, stoned, and cut into 1-centimetre (⅜-inch) chunks
- 10 blueberries, halved if large
- 1 teaspoon honey, plus extra to drizzle

Cooking tools

- Mixing bowl
- 2 sealable jars with lids

1 Combine the yogurt and milk with the oats and chia seeds in a mixing bowl. Mix in the chopped peach and blueberries, folding them gently to keep the pieces whole (see Chef's tip, right).

2 Spoon the oaty yogurt mix between two jars. Seal with a lid and leave in the fridge overnight.

3 In the morning, when you're ready for breakfast, drizzle a little honey over the oats. Now eat them straight from the jar!

Chef's tip

To **fold in the fruit**, scoop from the bottom and **lift up to the top**.

MAKES 8
large or 16 small

 15 prep
10 cook

Ingredients

For the blueberry syrup
- 100 grams (3½ ounces) blueberries
- 2 tablespoons water
- 1 tablespoon honey

For the pancakes
- 1 egg
- 3 cooked beetroots (about 230 grams/8 ounces)
- 2 tablespoons sunflower oil
- 150 millilitres (5 fluid ounces) low-fat (semi-skimmed) milk
- 160 grams (5¾ ounces) wholemeal flour
- 1½ teaspoons baking powder

For Abby Cadabby's face
- ½ small banana, sliced
- 6 blueberries, halved
- 1 strawberry, sliced

Cooking tools
- Mixing bowl
- Blender
- Whisk
- Non-stick frying pan
- Spatula

Zip-Zap Pancakes

These light and airy fairy pancakes are great for a **family brunch**. Everyone can **decorate their own pancake** with a different expression for **Abby Cadabby**!

1 Put the blueberries in a small pan with the water and honey. Heat over medium heat for 4–5 minutes, until the blueberries start to burst and the mixture thickens a little. Remove from the heat and put aside.

2 Separate the egg, breaking the white into a large mixing bowl. Add the egg yolk, 1 tablespoon oil, and the remaining pancake ingredients to a blender. Blend until smooth.

3 Beat the egg white into soft peaks with a hand whisk for about 5 minutes. Carefully push the egg white to one side of the mixing bowl. Pour in the mixture from the blender. Gently fold the two together into a smooth, fluffy batter.

4 Heat a little oil in a non-stick pan over medium heat. Spoon a dollop of the batter, about 2 tablespoons, into the pan.

5 Once bubbles start to appear on the surface of the pancake, flip it over with a spatula to cook the other side for 1–2 minutes more. Use the remaining batter to make more pancakes.

6 Serve one pancake in the centre of the plate. Make eyes from banana and blueberry slices. Use strawberry slices for Abby's nose and mouth. Spoon some blueberry syrup for hair.

7 Any remaining pancakes can be cooled and frozen in a sealed bag for up to 3 months.

Helping hand

Help **count and measure out** the pancake ingredients to put into the **blender**.

Fruity French Toast

These soft, warm, banana-flavoured **French toast slices** are soaked in egg and lightly fried. A crunchy **sprinkle of toasted coconut** adds a tropical taste that will **give you a sunny feeling**, whatever the weather.

SERVES 2

10 prep
15 cook

Ingredients
- 2 eggs
- 1 large ripe banana, peeled and cut in half
- A pinch of ground cinnamon
- ½ teaspoon vanilla extract
- 4 tablespoons low-fat (semi-skimmed) milk
- 2 slices wholemeal bread
- Sunflower oil
- 2 tablespoons unsweetened dried, desiccated coconut, toasted

Cooking tools
- Large shallow bowl
- Fork and bowl
- Whisk
- Non-stick frying pan
- Spatula

1 Break the eggs into a large shallow bowl. Lightly beat with a fork so that the yolk and white are mixed.

2 In a small bowl, mash half the banana with a clean fork. Add the mashed banana to the beaten egg along with the cinnamon and vanilla. Mix together with a fork.

3 Pour in the milk and use a whisk to mix everything together. Dip one slice of bread into the eggy mixture. Turn over to coat both sides.

4 Warm a large non-stick pan over medium heat with a drizzle of sunflower oil. Carefully lay the first slice of soaked bread into the hot pan. Cook for 4 minutes, or until golden.

5 Use a spatula to flip the slice of bread over and cook the other side until golden. Transfer to a serving plate. Dip and cook the second slice of bread in the same way. Add a little extra oil to the pan to stop it from sticking, if necessary.

6 When you're ready to eat, slice up the remaining half of the banana. Cut each piece of toast into fingers. Sprinkle the toast with the banana slices and a pinch of toasted coconut.

* * * * * * * * * * * * * * * * *

Chocolatey Porridge

Start your day with a **bowl of porridge**, **just like Elmo**. This recipe uses cocoa powder to **turn the porridge chocolatey**. The fresh raspberries give a **zingy taste** that will wake up your tastebuds.

 SERVES 2

 5 prep
10 cook

Ingredients
- 8 tablespoons porridge oats
- 1 teaspoon flaxseeds
- 1½ teaspoons unsweetened cocoa powder
- 200 millilitres (7 fluid ounces) low-fat (semi-skimmed) milk
- 2 teaspoons honey
- 10 raspberries

Cooking tools
- Small saucepan
- Wooden spoon

1 Add the oats, flaxseeds, cocoa powder, and milk to a small pan. Cook over a low heat, stirring all the time with a wooden spoon for about 5–10 minutes, until the porridge is thick and creamy.

2 Add just enough of the honey, a little at a time, to make it sweet enough. Divide between 2 bowls. Add 5 raspberries to each bowl and leave to cool slightly before serving.

Helping hand

Get counting! Sort the 10 raspberries into **2 piles** before adding them to the cooked porridge.

✦✦✦✦✦✦✦✦✦✦✦✦✦✦✦✦✦✦

Super Grover Smoothie

Start the day with **Grover's smiley face**! You can supercharge the colour of this low-sugar smoothie with **blue spirulina**, a powder made from an algae. It is full of healthy **nutrients** and **vitamins**.

 SERVES 1

 10 prep

Ingredients
- A handful of sliced blueberries (about 40 grams/1¼ ounces), plus extra to serve
- ¼ small avocado, peeled and stoned
- 4 tablespoons low-fat (semi-skimmed) milk
- 2 tablespoons porridge oats
- 2 tablespoons low-fat Greek yogurt
- 1 teaspoon blue spirulina powder, optional
- 1 strawberry

For Grover's face
- 2 banana slices
- 1 blueberry, halved
- ½ strawberry

Cooking tools
- Blender

1 Pulse the blueberries in a blender a few times to form a puree. Spoon out 2 tablespoons of puree and set aside in a bowl.

2 Add the remaining smoothie ingredients to the blender. Blend until smooth.

3 Pour the smoothie mix into a shallow serving bowl and get decorating.

4 For Grover's face, use banana slices and blueberry halves for his eyes. Make his nose with half a strawberry.

5 Now create a mouth with the blueberry puree you saved in step 1. Eat straight away!

HEALTHY HABITS

Why not make every Saturday a homemade **Smoothie Saturday**?

★ ★ ★ ★ ★ ★ ★ ★ ★ ★ ★ ★ ★ ★ ★ ★ ★ ★

Gonger's Egg Surprise

Eggs and toast are **great for breakfast** but have you tried **eggs IN toast**? Choose a cookie cutter in a simple shape, such as a circle, triangle, or square, and **stamp out a hole to hold the egg** as it cooks.

 SERVES 2

 **5 prep
10 cook**

Ingredients
- 2 slices wholemeal bread
- 2 teaspoons olive oil
- 2 tablespoons chopped, wilted spinach
- 2 eggs
- ½ avocado, peeled, stoned, and cut into slices, to serve

Cooking tools
- Cookie cutter, about 8 centimetres (3 inches) diameter
- Large non-stick frying pan with lid
- Small bowl
- Spatula

1 Use the cookie cutter to stamp a hole out of the centre of each slice of bread. Keep the cut-out piece.

2 Heat a teaspoon of oil in a large non-stick pan over low–medium heat. Add the slices of bread and cut-outs to the pan. Fry for about 3–4 minutes, or until the bread is golden brown. Flip over using a spatula. Add more oil if necessary to stop the bread sticking.

3 Divide the chopped spinach between each slice of bread. Spread it out in the middle of each cut-out hole and around the edges.

4 Crack an egg into a bowl, keeping the yolk whole. Carefully pour the egg on top of the spinach in the hole. Do the same to pour the second egg into the hole in the other slice of bread.

5 Cover the pan for 4–5 minutes, until the egg white is cooked through and the yolk is still runny.

6 Use a spatula to lift out the cut-out pieces and put on a plate. Top with slices of avocado. Lift each slice of egg-filled toast onto the plates and serve.

Helping hand

Push the **cookie cutter** into the bread to make a hole. Try other shapes, too. A **round egg in a square hole** looks cool!

* * * * * * * * * * * * * * * * *

Toast 'n' Beans

A **hungry tummy** in the morning will be a **happy tummy** after some **homemade beans**. Help to sort all the ingredients before you start – **how many red ingredients do you need**?

 SERVES 4

 **5 prep
20 cook**

Ingredients
- 1 tablespoon olive oil
- 1 small red onion, finely chopped
- ½ red bell pepper, finely chopped
- 1 garlic clove, crushed
- 1 tablespoon tomato puree
- 1 teaspoon smoked paprika
- 200 millilitres (7 fluid ounces) passata with basil
- 400-gram (14-ounce) can mixed beans, drained and rinsed
- ½ teaspoon balsamic vinegar
- 4 slices wholemeal bread or wholemeal English muffins, toasted

Cooking tools
- Saucepan
- Wooden spoon
- Toaster

1 Heat the olive oil in a saucepan over medium heat. Add the onion, pepper, and garlic. Cook for 4–5 minutes until the onions begin to soften.

2 Add the tomato puree and paprika, stir, and cook for 2 more minutes.

3 Pour in the passata, the drained beans, and the balsamic vinegar. Bring to a simmer and cook for 10 minutes, stirring gently a few times.

4 Let cool a little and serve with toast or toasted muffins. Any leftovers can be stored in an airtight container in the fridge for up to 3 days.

HEALTHY HABITS

Get in the habit of **storing leftovers** for another day rather than throwing them in the bin.

Om-Nom Omelette Cups

These little baked omelettes are full of **yummy** mushrooms and spinach. **A sprinkle of cheese** on top makes them even tastier! If you don't eat them all at once, they make **a great snack** for later.

SERVES 6

**10 prep
25 cook**

Ingredients
- 2 tablespoons olive oil
- 6 baby button mushrooms, sliced (about 50 grams/ 1¾ ounces)
- 2 spring onions, sliced
- 2 handfuls of baby spinach (40 grams/1¼ ounces)
- 5 eggs
- 2 tablespoons low-fat (semi-skimmed) milk
- 2 tablespoons grated Parmesan cheese

Cooking tools
- 6-hole muffin tin
- Non-stick frying pan with lid
- Whisk
- Jug

1 Preheat the oven to 190°C (170°C fan/375°F/Gas 5). Use 1 tablespoon of olive oil on a sheet of kitchen paper to lightly grease six holes of a muffin tin.

2 Heat the remaining oil in a non-stick pan over medium heat. Add the mushrooms and spring onions. Fry for 5 minutes until slightly coloured and softened. Tip them onto a plate and set aside.

3 Add the spinach to the same pan. Cover with a lid and cook for 1–2 minutes, until the leaves have wilted.

4 Remove the spinach to a plate lined with kitchen paper. Place a sheet of kitchen paper on top and squeeze the spinach dry. Then roughly chop.

(Recipe continues on the next page)

5 Beat the eggs and milk together in a jug. Divide the cooled veggies between the muffin tin holes. Pour over the eggs and sprinkle each with a little Parmesan.

Chef's tip

Swap in your **favourite veggies**, such as grated courgettes or sliced peppers.

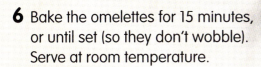

6 Bake the omelettes for 15 minutes, or until set (so they don't wobble). Serve at room temperature.

7 Store any remaining omelettes in an airtight container in the fridge for up to 3 days.

41

SUPER SNACKS

★ ★ ★ ★ ★ ★ ★ ★ ★ ★ ★ ★ ★ ★ ★ ★

Fruity Pops

These **pretty ice pops** will keep you cool with **bursts of blackberry, tropical kiwi, and coconut**. You can use other berries, too. Try squashing raspberries in the same way for a **zappy pink version**.

 MAKES 8

 40 prep
plus 8 hours freezing, or overnight

Ingredients
- 150 grams (5½ ounces) blackberries
- 100 millilitres (3½ fluid ounces) coconut water
- 3 ripe kiwis, peeled and roughly chopped

Cooking tools
- Mesh sieve
- Large bowl
- 8 ice pop moulds and sticks
- Blender

1 Put the blackberries in a sieve. Wash under running water. Lightly shake to get rid of any extra water.

2 To remove the seeds from the blackberries, rest the sieve over a large bowl. Use the back of a spoon to squash the berries through into the bowl below.

3 Scrape the bottom of the sieve to get every last bit of the berry flesh. Divide the squashed blackberries between the ice pop moulds. Freeze for 30 minutes.

4 Add the kiwi and coconut water to a blender. Pulse a few times to make a chunky puree.

5 Pour the kiwi mixture onto the frozen blackberry ice pop. Carefully push a stick into each mould.

6 Put the moulds back in the freezer for at least 8 hours, or overnight, until frozen solid. Once frozen, the ice pops will keep for up to 1 month.

7 When ready to eat, leave to thaw at room temperature for 10 minutes before removing from the moulds.

Helping hand

Squish the berries through the sieve to **separate the seeds**. Try it with raspberries, too!

MAKES 6

 **15 prep
20 cook**

Ingredients
- 80 grams (3 ounces) self-raising wholemeal flour
- 3 tablespoons caster sugar
- 60 grams (2 ounces) porridge oats
- 1 teaspoon ground cinnamon
- Zest of 1 small orange, plus extra to serve
- 1 egg, beaten
- 75 millilitres (2½ fluid ounces) low-fat (semi-skimmed) milk
- 2 tablespoons olive oil
- 100 grams (3½ ounces) grated carrot (about 2 carrots)

For the topping
- 3 tablespoons low-fat cream cheese
- 1 teaspoon maple syrup
- 1 tablespoon freshly squeezed orange juice

Cooking tools
- 6-hole muffin tin
- Mixing bowl
- Paper or silicone muffin liners
- Whisk
- Wire rack

Tip-Top Muffins

Orange adds a wonderful flavour to these **moist carrot and oat muffins**. They are made even more special if little chefs help **squeeze** the juice!

1 Preheat the oven to 200°C (180°C fan/400°F/Gas 6). Line a 6-hole muffin tin with muffin liners.

2 In a mixing bowl, stir together the flour, sugar, oats, cinnamon, and zest.

3 In a separate bowl, use the whisk to beat together the egg, milk, and oil. Pour the milk mixture over the dry ingredients.

4 Add the carrot and fold everything together until just combined. Divide the batter between the muffin liners.

5 Bake for 18–20 minutes, until risen and golden. Cool in the tin for 5 minutes. Remove to a wire rack to cool completely.

6 Beat the cream cheese with the maple syrup and the orange juice until smooth. Put a dollop of the topping on each muffin just before you eat them and sprinkle with a little more orange zest, if you like.

7 The muffins can be stored for up to 3 days in an airtight container at room temperature. Store the topping in the fridge for up to 3 days.

Helping hand

Get your whisk at the ready to stir, stir, stir and mix up the egg, milk, and oil.

★★★★★★★★★★★★★★★★

Veggie Pots to Go!

Chop up **crunchy veggie sticks** to scoop out the creamy dip made from mashed avocado and yogurt. This snack is **great for day trips**, or for making two and sharing with **your best friend**.

 SERVES 2

 10 prep

Ingredients
- 1 small, ripe avocado, stoned
- 2 teaspoons freshly squeezed lime juice
- 1 tablespoon low-fat Greek yogurt
- 3 cherry tomatoes, quartered
- A pinch of smoked paprika
- 1 carrot, peeled and cut into sticks
- ¼ cucumber, peeled and cut into sticks
- ⅓ red bell pepper, cut into sticks

Cooking tools
- Fork and bowl
- 2 jars with lids or sealable food storage pots

1 Scoop the avocado flesh out of the skins. Use a fork to mash the avocado and lime juice together in a bowl.

2 Stir the yogurt, chopped tomatoes, and paprika into the mashed avocado.

3 Spoon the yogurt and avocado mixture into the jars. Add a mix of veggie sticks to each jar.

4 Screw on the jar lids, ready to take on an outing or to enjoy at home.

HEALTHY HABITS

At the shops, head to the **veggie aisle** to choose the **tasty ingredients** for your snack!

✳ ✳ ✳ ✳ ✳ ✳ ✳ ✳ ✳ ✳ ✳ ✳ ✳ ✳ ✳ ✳ ✳ ✳

Count von Count's Oatcakes

Mix, **roll**, and **stamp** to make these crunchy, cheesy oatcakes.
Using **number cookie cutters** means you get to make delicious food
and **count at the same time**. Ah, ah, ah!

 MAKES ABOUT 28

 15 prep
15 cook

Ingredients
- 120 grams (4½ ounces) porridge oats
- 50 grams (1¾ ounces) grated low-salt Cheddar cheese
- 1 tablespoon olive oil
- 5 tablespoons warm water
- 1 tablespoon wholemeal flour, for dusting

Cooking tools
- Food processor
- Mixing bowl
- Rolling pin
- Cookie cutters
- 2 baking sheets lined with baking parchment
- Wire rack

1 Preheat the oven to 200°C (180°C fan/400°F/Gas 6). Add the oats to a food processor. Pulse until it looks like rough flour.

2 Transfer the oat flour to a mixing bowl along with the grated cheese. Pour the oil over the mixture with the warm water.

3 Mix well until everything comes together into a sticky dough. Dust the worktop with a little flour. Roll out the dough to a thickness of about 3 millimetres (⅛ inch).

4 Using number cookie cutters (or any shape you like), stamp out shapes from the dough. Put the shapes on the lined baking sheets as you go.

5 Bake for 12–15 minutes, until the edges of the oatcakes are starting to brown.

6 Remove from the oven. Leave to cool on the sheets for a few minutes. Transfer to a wire rack to cool completely.

7 Store in an airtight container for up to 1 week.

Chef's tip

Dip the **cookie cutter** in some **flour** before you stamp. This stops it from **getting stuck** in the dough.

★ ★ ★ ★ ★ ★ ★ ★ ★ ★ ★ ★ ★ ★ ★ ★ ★ ★

Sweet Stars

These no-cook snacks are made using **star shapes**, but you can use **any shape cookie cutter** you like. Just mix up some raspberries with healthy oats, then have fun rolling and cutting out to make **yummy snacks to share**.

MAKES 20

**15 prep
10 chill**

Ingredients
- 80 grams (3 ounces) raspberries
- 65 grams (2¼ ounces) porridge oats
- 40 grams (1¼ ounces) unsweetened, dried desiccated coconut
- 1 tablespoon maple syrup
- 1 teaspoon chia seeds
- 1 teaspoon ground flaxseeds
- ¼ teaspoon vanilla extract

Cooking tools
- Food processor
- 2 sheets of baking parchment
- Rolling pin
- Shallow dish
- Cookie cutter

1 Put the raspberries, oats, half the coconut (20 grams/ ¾ ounce), and the rest of the ingredients into a food processor. Blend into a smooth, sticky dough.

2 Put the dough mix on a large sheet of baking parchment. Cover with a second sheet of parchment. Flatten with a rolling pin to make a disc about 1.5 centimetres (½ inch) thick. Chill for 10 minutes.

3 Put the remaining coconut in a shallow dish. Use a shaped cookie cutter, like a star, to press out shapes from the chilled dough.

4 Gently press the cut-out shape into the dish of coconut. Make sure that both sides of the shape are covered.

5 Roll any scraps of the raspberry mixture into balls of about 1 teaspoon in size. Roll the balls in the coconut.

6 Store in an airtight container in the fridge for up to 2 days. You can also freeze them for up to 1 month.

Chef's tip

For a **different flavour**, swap
the raspberries for **blueberries**.
Coat with blitzed
sunflower seeds.

★ ★ ★ ★ ★ ★ ★ ★ ★ ★ ★ ★ ★ ★ ★ ★ ★ ★

Big Bird Sunshine Dip

This **tangy sweet potato hummus** makes the perfect base for shaping **Big Bird's face**. Add breadsticks and pepper slices for his feathers to make a most **remarkable sharing plate for snack time**!

 SERVES 2–3

 **15 prep
5 cook**

Ingredients
For the Sunshine Dip
- 1 small sweet potato (about 100 grams/3½ ounces)
- 150 grams (5½ ounces) canned chickpeas, drained and rinsed
- 1 tablespoon olive oil or tahini
- ½ small garlic clove
- Freshly squeezed juice of ½ small lemon
- ¼ teaspoon ground turmeric
- 100 millilitres (3½ fluid ounces) water

For Big Bird's face
- 5 wholemeal breadsticks, halved
- 1 yellow bell pepper, sliced
- 1 tomato
- 2 slices of cucumber
- 2 slices of pitted black olive

Cooking tools
- Microwave
- Blender

1 Carefully prick the skin of the sweet potato all over with a fork and place on a plate. Microwave on high for 5 minutes or until tender. Slice down the middle and leave to cool.

2 Scoop out the flesh from the cooled sweet potato with a spoon. Add it to a blender. Throw away the skin or put it in the compost.

3 Add the chickpeas, olive oil or tahini, garlic, lemon juice, and turmeric to the blender. Pulse for 1 minute to combine all the ingredients.

4 Add about 50 millilitres (2 fluid ounces) water. Blend again for one more minute, adding the remaining water as needed to achieve a smooth, thick consistency.

5 Spoon half the hummus out onto a dinner plate. Make an oval shape with the back of the spoon.

6 Now make Big Bird! Arrange breadsticks and pepper slices around the hummus to make his feathers.

7 Use a wider, triangular piece of pepper and cut some thin slices of tomato for a beak. Use slices of cucumber, quarter slices of tomato, and olive slices for eyes.

8 Any remaining dip will store in an airtight container in the fridge for up to 4 days.

HEALTHY HABITS

Sharing plates are a great idea for getting **everyone together** around the table.

Mini Monster Muffins

These muffins are brought to you by the **colour green**! Sweetened **with bananas** and topped with blueberries, they make a **delicious treat for picnics** with friends.

 MAKES 24

 **15 prep
20 cook**

Ingredients
- 90 grams (3¼ ounces) porridge oats
- 140 grams (5 ounces) wholemeal self-raising flour
- 1 teaspoon baking powder
- 1 teaspoon ground cinnamon
- 2 bananas, roughly chopped (about 75 grams/6 ounces)
- 100 grams (3½ ounces) frozen spinach, defrosted
- 3 tablespoons sunflower oil
- 120 millilitres (4 fluid ounces) low-fat (semi-skimmed) milk
- 2 tablespoons maple syrup or honey
- 1 egg
- 48 blueberries

Cooking tools
- 24-hole mini muffin tin
- Mini muffin liners
- Large mixing bowl
- Food processor
- Wire rack

1 Preheat the oven to 190°C (170°C fan/375°F/Gas 5). Line the holes of the muffin tiin with muffin liners.

2 Combine the oats, flour, baking powder, and ground cinnamon in a large mixing bowl.

3 Put the banana, spinach, oil, milk, maple syrup or honey, and egg in the bowl of a food processor. Blend into a green, smooth mixture.

4 Pour the mixture over the dry ingredients. Fold everything together into a smooth batter, making sure there are no pockets of flour.

5 Fill each prepared muffin liner with the batter. Push 2 blueberries into the top of each muffin. Bake for 15–20 minutes.

6 Cool in the tin for 10 minutes. Transfer to a wire rack to cool completely.

7 Store in an airtight container for 2–3 days or freeze for up to 1 month.

Helping hand

Use a teaspoon to scoop **dollops of batter** into the **muffin liners**. Are they filled to the **same level**?

* * * * * * * * * * * * * * * *

Granola Cookie Bites

These **crunchy oat cookies** have a **sticky pear surprise inside**. They would probably be a favourite snack for both **Cookie Monster** and **Bert**. Will they be one of **your best-loved treats**, too?

 MAKES 10

 **10 prep
15 cook**

Ingredients
- 100 grams (3½ ounces) porridge oats
- ½ teaspoon ground cinnamon
- 1 tablespoon chia seeds
- 4 tablespoons low-fat (semi-skimmed) milk
- 1 ripe pear, peeled and grated (about 150 grams/ 5½ ounces)
- 2 tablespoons wholemeal flour
- 3 tablespoons sunflower oil
- 1 tablespoon maple syrup

Cooking tools
- Mixing bowl
- Baking sheet lined with baking parchment
- Wire rack

1 Preheat the oven to 180°C (160°C fan/350°F/Gas 4).

2 Combine the oats, cinnamon, and chia seeds in a mixing bowl. Pour over the milk. Stir to coat everything. Leave to stand for 5 minutes.

3 Fold the remaining ingredients through to mix everything in. Spoon the mixture into 10 heaped rounds on the baking sheet. Press down gently on each round to flatten it slightly (see Chef's tip, right).

4 Bake for 12–15 minutes, until the cookies are golden and slightly crisp on top. Transfer to a wire rack.

5 The cookies can be served warm or cold. Store in an airtight container for up to 5 days.

Chef's tip

Wet your hands before flattening the **heaped rounds** so they don't stick to you.

YUMMY LUNCHES

★ ★ ★ ★ ★ ★ ★ ★ ★ ★ ★ ★ ★ ★ ★

 SERVES 2

 **5 prep
15 cook**

Ingredients
- 40 grams (1¼ ounces) self-raising wholemeal flour
- ¼ teaspoon baking powder
- 1 egg, beaten
- 1 teaspoon olive oil
- 100 grams (3½ ounces) low-fat cottage cheese
- 1 small sweet potato (about 50 grams/1¾ ounces), peeled and coarsely grated
- 1 tablespoon chopped basil

For the salsa
- 60 grams (2 ounces) cucumber, peeled and cut into 1-centimetre (⅜-inch) dice
- 4 cherry tomatoes, quartered
- 2 tablespoons chopped basil
- Zest and freshly squeezed juice of ½ lime

Cooking tools
- Waffle iron
- Food processor
- Wire rack

Wonder Waffles

These super-tasty waffles are made with a **super ingredient** – sweet potato! Full of vitamins, they will give you energy **all day**.

1 Preheat the waffle iron while you prepare the batter.

2 Add the flour and baking powder to a food processor. Pour in the beaten egg, the oil, and half the cottage cheese (50 grams/1¾ ounces).

3 Blend until you have a silky batter. Stir in the grated sweet potato and chopped basil.

4 Spoon the mixture between the two waffle plates. Seal and cook for 10 minutes or until crisp and golden. Transfer to a wire rack while you make the salsa.

5 For the salsa, mix the cucumber, tomatoes, basil, and lime juice and zest all together.

6 Serve one waffle each. Put a dollop of the remaining cottage cheese and some salsa on the top.

Grouch on Toast

A mix of **smashed avocado** and **hardboiled egg** makes a tasty toast spread. Use eggy eyes and an olive mouth to make Oscar's face. Is he **grouchy** or **happy** today?

 SERVES 2

 5 prep
15 cook

Ingredients
- 2 eggs
- 2 slices wholemeal bread
- ½ small avocado, peeled and stoned
- 4 cherry tomatoes, chopped
- ½ lemon
- 8 slices pitted black olives

Cooking tools
- Saucepan
- Plate and fork
- Toaster

1 Add the eggs to a saucepan of boiling water and boil for 9 minutes. Plunge the eggs into cold water. Leave to cool for 5 minutes before peeling.

2 Mash the peeled avocado flesh on a plate with the back of a fork. Add a squeeze of lemon juice. Stir through the chopped tomatoes.

3 Toast the bread slices until golden. Cut 2 slices lengthways from the middle of each peeled egg. Put these aside to make Oscar's eyes later.

4 Roughly chop the leftover egg and add it to the avocado mix. Divide the mix between the slices of toast.

5 Use the back of the fork to fluff the avocado to look like Oscar's fur. Add the egg slices to make eyes. Put an olive slice in the middle of each eye for the pupils.

6 Use the remaining olives to make Oscar's eyebrows and mouth. Eat straight away before anyone gets grouchy for lunch!

Helping hand

Help **squeeze the lemon** juice over the **avocado** to stop it from turning brown.

✦ ✦ ✦ ✦ ✦ ✦ ✦ ✦ ✦ ✦ ✦ ✦ ✦ ✦ ✦ ✦ ✦ ✦

Q is for Quesadilla!

These **tasty quesadillas** are full of squashed beans and oozy cheese. Their shape makes them **perfect for little hands** to **hold and dip** into the tangy yogurt and chive sauce.

 SERVES 2

 10 prep
15 cook

Ingredients
- 80 grams (3 ounces) black beans, drained and rinsed
- ¼ teaspoon smoked paprika
- 2 wholemeal or whole-wheat tortilla wraps
- 40 grams (1¼ ounces) grated low-salt Cheddar cheese
- ⅓ red bell pepper, diced
- 2 tablespoons low-fat Greek yogurt
- ½ teaspoon snipped chives, optional
- Cucumber sticks, peeled, to serve

Cooking tools
- Shallow bowl
- Fork or masher
- Large non-stick frying pan
- Spatula

1 Add the black beans to a shallow bowl. Sprinkle over the paprika. Use a fork or masher to roughly mash the beans.

2 Lay the wraps out flat and divide the mashed beans between them. Spread the beans out to cover half of each wrap.

3 Sprinkle the beans with the cheese and diced pepper. Fold each wrap in half to form a semicircle.

4 Warm a large non-stick pan over medium heat. Dry-fry one quesadilla for 3–4 minutes, until golden and the cheese has started to melt.

5 Use a spatula to flip the quesadilla to cook the other side for 2 more minutes. Remove from the pan. Cook the second quesadilla. Leave to cool while you make the dip.

6 Divide the yogurt between serving plates and sprinkle with snipped chives, if you like.

7 Cut each quesadilla into 4 triangles. Serve with the yogurt dip and some sticks of cucumber.

Helping hand

Take a **big pinch of cheese** to sprinkle in the wrap. Look for **shapes**, such as circles and triangles, as you cook.

★★★★★★★★★★★★★★★★

Roll and Go Wraps

These little wraps are **full of delicious roast chicken** and crunchy salad, rolled up in a basil and cream cheese filling. **They are perfect to pack** as a healthy lunch if you're on the go!

 SERVES 2

 15 prep

Ingredients

- 75 grams (2½ ounces) cold roasted chicken breast, shredded
- 1 teaspoon finely chopped basil
- 2 tablespoons low-fat cream cheese
- 2 mini wholemeal or whole-wheat tortilla wraps
- 4 cherry tomatoes, quartered
- ¼ cucumber, peeled and cut into sticks

Cooking tools

- Mixing bowl

1 Mix the chicken, basil, and cream cheese together in a bowl.

2 Lay the wraps out flat and divide the chicken mixture between them. Spread it in a line down the middle of each one. Top with the tomato and cucumber pieces.

3 Fold in the sides and roll up the wraps tightly. Press down firmly. Cut in half across the middle to serve.

HEALTHY HABITS

Serve with **some extra veggies**, such as cherry tomatoes or broccoli, **on the side**.

* * * * * * * * * * * * * * * * *

Fluffy Fritters

Speckled with **green herbs** and **whole sweetcorn kernels**, these lightly fried fritters make a filling lunch. Serve with some **smashed avocado** for scooping.

 SERVES 2

 **5 prep
15 cook**

Ingredients
- 100 grams (3½ ounces) canned sweetcorn kernels, drained, or frozen and thawed
- 1 egg
- 3 tablespoons self-raising wholemeal flour
- 1 tablespoon low-fat (semi-skimmed) milk
- ¼ teaspoon smoked paprika
- 1 tablespoon snipped chives
- 1 teaspoon olive oil
- ½ small avocado, peeled and stoned
- 4 cherry tomatoes, halved, to serve

Cooking tools
- Food processor
- Large non-stick frying pan
- Spatula
- Bowl and fork

1 Put 2 tablespoons of sweetcorn in a bowl and tip the rest of the kernels into a food processor with all the other ingredients, except the avocado and tomatoes.

2 Blend into a rough batter – mix them up! Stir through the remaining sweetcorn.

3 Warm a large non-stick pan over medium heat. Spoon 2 tablespoons of batter for each fritter into the pan. Cook 2 fritters at a time.

4 After 2 minutes, flip the fritters over with a spatula and cook for another 2 minutes until fluffy and golden. Remove from the pan. Make 2 more fritters with the remaining batter.

5 Leave the fritters to cool slightly while you mash the avocado. Put the avocado in a bowl and smoosh it with the back of a fork.

6 Top the fritters with some smashed avocado and serve alongside a few tomato halves.

Chef's tip

Experiment with **flavour**.
Try a different herb, like
parsley or **tarragon**.

* * * * * * * * * * * * * * * * *

Mix and Match Mini Kebabs

With **bite-sized** pieces of **juicy chicken and veggies,** these mini kebabs are perfect for little hands to hold. **Mix and match** what goes on each skewer as you thread them up.

 SERVES 2

 **5 prep
15 cook**

Ingredients
- 1 skinless chicken thigh fillet (about 50 grams/ 1¾ ounces)
- Freshly squeezed juice and zest of ½ lemon
- 1 teaspoon mixed herbs
- 2 cherry tomatoes, halved
- ¼ yellow bell pepper, cut into bite-sized chunks
- 2 teaspoons olive oil
- 1 wholemeal pitta
- 2 tablespoons Sunshine Dip (see page 54)

Cooking tools
- 2 small pre-soaked wooden skewers, sharp ends removed
- Basting brush
- Toaster

1 Preheat the grill to high.

2 Cut the chicken into 6 bite-sized chunks. Squeeze over the lemon juice. Sprinkle with the herbs and lemon zest and mix together.

3 Thread 3 pieces of chicken onto each skewer with the pieces of tomato and pepper in between. Brush each skewer with olive oil.

4 Place under the grill for 10–12 minutes, turning regularly. Check the chicken is thoroughly cooked. Leave to cool a little.

5 While the chicken is cooking, lightly toast the pitta. Split it in half and fill each half with a spoonful of Sunshine Dip. Serve each skewer with a filled pitta half.

👋 Helping hand

Get **scooping** and **filling** the pitta halves **with the dip** while the kebabs are cooking.

★★★★★★★★★★★★★★★★

Quick Quiche

Bursting with yumminess, these little quiches are full of veggies, all wrapped up in a toasty tortilla. **Eat them hot or cold**. This is a great way to use up any **leftover veggies** you have in the fridge.

 SERVES 2

 5 prep 15 cook

Ingredients
- 1 wholemeal or whole-wheat tortilla wrap
- 2 cherry tomatoes, quartered
- 40 grams (1¼ ounces) broccoli, lightly steamed and cut into small florets
- 1 spring onion, finely sliced
- 2 large eggs
- 1 tablespoon low-fat (semi-skimmed) milk
- 1 teaspoon freshly grated Parmesan cheese
- Sticks of raw veggies, to serve

Cooking tools
- Pie dish, about 10 x 15 centimetres (4 x 6 inches)
- Bowl
- Whisk

1 Preheat the oven to 200°C (180°C fan/400°F/Gas 6).

2 Press the tortilla wrap into a pie dish. Scatter in the tomatoes, broccoli, and spring onion.

3 Crack the eggs into a bowl and lightly whisk them together with the milk. Pour over the veg and top with grated Parmesan.

4 Bake in the oven for 15 minutes until set (so it doesn't wobble) and slightly puffed up.

5 Leave to cool before serving with sticks or slices of raw veggies, called crudités.

Helping hand

Help fill the tortilla wrap with the **prepared vegetables**. Spread them out evenly.

Springy Spring Rolls

Crunchy pepper and cucumber, **yummy tuna**, silky noodles, and tangy mayo are all wrapped up together in these soft **spring rolls**. Help out **rolling them up** to learn a new **chef's skill**.

 SERVES 2

 **15 prep
5 cook**

Ingredients

- 70 grams (2½ ounces) canned tuna in spring water, drained
- 2 teaspoons low-fat mayonnaise
- ⅓ cucumber (about 60 grams/2 ounces), peeled and cut into thin strips
- ¼ yellow bell pepper (about 40 grams/1¼ ounces)
- 1 teaspoon chopped coriander, optional
- 50 grams (1¾ ounces) uncooked fine rice noodles
- 4 rice paper wrappers (Vietnamese spring roll wrappers)

Cooking tools

- Strainer
- Scissors
- Chopping board

1 Mix the tuna with the mayonnaise and set aside. Set out the cucumber, pepper slices, and chopped coriander, if using, ready to assemble the rolls.

2 Cook the noodles following the packet instructions. Drain and rinse under cold water. Chop up the noodles using scissors.

(Recipe continues on the next page)

3 Lay out a sheet of damp kitchen paper on a chopping board. Soak a rice paper sheet in hot water until soft. Carefully lay it out as flat as possible on the damp kitchen paper.

4 Spoon a quarter of the tuna in a line across the centre. Leave a 2-centimetre (¾-inch) wide border on each side.

5 Top the tuna with a quarter of the veggie strips, a portion of the noodles, and a sprinkle of coriander.

Chef's tip

Roll the wrapper away from you, **tucking** the filling together **tightly inside** as you roll.

6 Fold the sides in over the filling. Tuck the bottom of the rice paper fully over the filling. Roll up so everything is kept neatly inside (see Chef's tip, above).

7 Do the same again with the 3 remaining rice paper sheets. Slice each roll in half and dig in.

79

DELICIOUS DINNERS

SERVES 2

 **10 prep
35 cook**

Ingredients

- 1 teaspoon chopped mint
- 2 tablespoons low-fat Greek yogurt
- 2 tablespoons grated cucumber
- 60 grams (2 ounces) lean minced lamb
- ¼ small red onion, finely chopped
- 1 small garlic clove, crushed
- A pinch each of ground cinnamon and ground cumin
- 1 teaspoon chopped flat-leaf parsley
- 80 grams (2¾ ounces) pre-cooked quinoa

For the roast vegetables

- ½ small sweet potato, peeled and cut into bite-sized chunks
- ¼ red bell pepper, cut into bite-sized chunks
- ½ small courgette, cut into semicircles
- 2 teaspoons olive oil

Cooking tools

- Baking sheet
- 4 pre-soaked mini wooden skewers, sharp ends removed
- Non-stick frying pan

Little Lamb Sticks

Discover **lots of flavours** and a fun way to eat with these **smoky** and **spicy** lamb koftas that are easy to dip in the minty sauce. Try threading the **roast veggies** on sticks, too.

1 Preheat the oven to 180°C (160°C fan/350°F/Gas 4). Spread the chopped veggies out on a baking sheet. Drizzle over the olive oil. Roast in the oven for about 20 minutes until tender.

2 While the veggies are roasting, make the dip. Mix the mint, yogurt, and cucumber together. Put to one side.

3 For the lamb koftas, combine the lamb, onion, garlic, parsley, and spices with 2 tablespoons of the quinoa.

4 Divide the mixture into 4 equal portions. Use your palms to shape each portion into an oval around the end of a skewer, just like a maraca!

5 Heat a dry non-stick pan over medium–high heat. Cook 2 koftas at a time. Turn regularly until golden on all sides and cooked through, about 10 minutes. Remove from the pan and leave to cool slightly.

6 Warm the remaining quinoa in the pan, adding a splash of water if it looks dry or is sticking. Serve the koftas with the quinoa, some roasted veggies, and a dollop of cucumber dip. Yum!

Helping hand

With clean hands, **squash and shape** the lamb mix around the wooden stick.

✴✴✴✴✴✴✴✴✴✴✴✴✴✴✴✴✴

Oodles of Noodles

A **bowl of noodles** topped with **honey-glazed salmon** is so yummy! Juicy flakes of salmon taste great but they also keep your body and brain healthy, so you can help the **Count to count**.

SERVES 2

**5 prep
15 cook**

Ingredients
- 1 salmon fillet, skin on (about 125 grams/4½ ounces), any bones removed (see Chef's tip, opposite)
- ½ teaspoon honey
- 2 teaspoon low-salt soy sauce
- 50 grams (1¾ ounces) dried medium egg noodles
- 12 mangetout, sliced
- 1 carrot, peeled and grated

Cooking tools
- Baking tin lined with aluminium foil
- Saucepan
- Fish tweezers

1 Preheat the oven to 200°C (180°C fan/400°F/Gas 6). Put the salmon fillet in the baking tin.

2 Mix the honey and soy sauce together. Pour over the salmon. Bake in the oven for 12 minutes or until cooked through. Leave to cool a little.

3 While the salmon is baking, cook the noodles following the packet instructions. Add the mangetout for the last minute of cooking.

4 Drain the noodles and mangetout. Divide between serving bowls along with the grated carrot.

5 Break the salmon into bite-sized pieces with a fork. Throw away the skin. Serve on top of the noodles with any cooking juices.

84

Chef's tip

Feel carefully for any fish bones. Use fish tweezers to hold the tip of the bone and **pull it out**.

✦ ✦ ✦ ✦ ✦ ✦ ✦ ✦ ✦ ✦ ✦ ✦ ✦ ✦ ✦ ✦ ✦ ✦

Coconutty Chicken Bites

This is a great recipe to **cook together**! Share out the tasks for **coating the bite-sized nuggets** of chicken and squash in a crispy coconut crumb.

 SERVES 2

 10 prep
15 cook

Ingredients
- 1 tablespoon olive oil
- 1 tablespoon unsweetened, dried desiccated coconut
- 6 tablespoons panko breadcrumbs
- 1 egg
- 1 tablespoon cornflour
- 80 grams (2¾ ounces) skinless chicken thigh fillet, cut into bite-sized chunks
- 50 grams (1¾ ounces) butternut squash, peeled and cut into 5-millimetre (¼-inch) thick semicircles
- Steamed baby potatoes and veggies, to serve

Cooking tools
- 3 shallow bowls
- Baking sheet lined with baking parchment
- Basting brush

1 Preheat the oven to 200°C (180°C fan/400°F/Gas 6). Brush the lined baking sheet with half the oil.

2 Line up 3 shallow bowls. In the first, mix the coconut and breadcrumbs together. In the second, beat the egg. Add the cornflour to the third bowl.

3 One by one, coat each piece of chicken and squash first in flour, then egg, and finally roll in the breadcrumb mix. Put the covered pieces on the prepared baking sheet as you go.

4 When all the nuggets are on the baking sheet, drizzle over the remaining oil. Bake in the centre of the oven for 12–15 minutes, until golden and cooked through. Carefully turn halfway through cooking.

5 Let the nuggets cool a little. Divide them equally between serving plates. Serve with steamed new potatoes and veggies of your choice.

Helping hand

Help out with **dusting**, **dipping**, and **rolling** the chicken and squash in breadcrumbs.

★★★★★★★★★★★★★★★★

Easy Peasy Pasta

This **green pasta sauce**, made from finely chopped **cooked spinach**, is super healthy and will help you to grow strong. Morsels of tasty roast chicken and tomatoes will keep **tummies happy**, too.

 SERVES 2

 **10 prep
40 cook**

Ingredients
- 85 grams (3 ounces) skinless chicken thigh fillet
- 4 cherry tomatoes, halved
- 1 tablespoon olive oil
- ½ small onion, chopped
- 1 garlic clove, chopped
- 2 large handfuls (about 60 grams/2 ounces) baby spinach
- 1 tablespoon grated Parmesan cheese, plus extra to serve
- ¼ teaspoon Dijon mustard, optional
- 100 grams (3½ ounces) wholemeal pasta

Cooking tools
- Baking tray
- Non-stick frying pan with lid
- Blender
- Saucepan

1 Preheat the oven to 190°C (170°C fan/375°F/Gas 5). Put the chicken fillet in a baking tray and roast for 10 minutes.

2 Add the cherry tomatoes to the baking tray and roast for another 10 minutes. Remove from the oven and leave to cool.

3 Heat the oil in a non-stick pan. Fry the onion and garlic for 5 minutes, until starting to soften.

4 Add the spinach to the frying pan, along with 2 tablespoons water. Cover and cook for a further minute, until the spinach has wilted.

5 Put the cooked spinach mix in a blender with another 2 tablespoons water, the Parmesan, and mustard, if using. Blend until smooth.

6 Cook the pasta following the packet instructions. Drain and return to the saucepan.

7 Shred the cooled chicken and add to the pasta. Pour over the spinach sauce and stir together so that everything is green!

8 Divide the pasta between serving bowls with the roast tomatoes on top and a sprinkle of Parmesan. Tuck in!

Chef's tip

To check that the **pasta** is cooked, cool a piece and give it **a bite**. Is it **hard or soft**?

Golden Goodness Fishcakes

Crispy on the **outside**, **fluffy** on the **inside**! These salmon fishcakes are **even yummier** if you try them with the **tangy tartare dip**. Squeeze some lemon over for **extra zingy flavour**.

 SERVES 2

 **15 prep
25 cook**

Ingredients
- 1 salmon fillet, skin on (about 125 grams/4½ ounces), any bones removed (see Chef's tip, page 85)
- 40 grams (1¼ ounces) broccoli florets
- 4 baby potatoes
- 1 tablespoon beaten egg
- 2 teaspoons olive oil
- Steamed veggies, to serve
- Lemon wedges, to serve

For the tartare dip
- 2 tablespoons low-fat Greek yogurt
- 1 cornichon, finely chopped
- 1 teaspoon snipped chives

Cooking tools
- Steamer saucepan
- Non-stick frying pan
- Spatula
- Bowl

1 Steam the salmon and broccoli over a pan of boiling water. Boil the potatoes in the pan below. This means you can cook everything in one pan at once. Cook for about 8–10 minutes.

2 When everything is cooked through, let it cool slightly. Use a fork to mash the potatoes in a bowl. Add the broccoli, breaking it up and mixing it all together.

3 Throw away the skin from the salmon. Break it into small flakes with the fork. Add the salmon flakes to the potato mix along with the beaten egg. Mash everything together.

4 Divide the mixture into 4 equal balls. Wet your hands and get squishing to flatten the balls into the shape of fishcakes.

5 Cook in two batches. Add a little olive oil to a non-stick pan over medium–high heat. Fry the fishcakes for 2–3 minutes. Use a spatula to flip the fishcakes and cook the other side for another 2–3 minutes.

6 Once the fishcakes are crisp and golden, transfer to the serving plates to cool.

7 Mix the tartare dip ingredients in a bowl. Serve with the fishcakes and some steamed veggies. Squeeze some lemon juice over before you tuck in.

Helping hand

Get **sticky** using your hands to knead and shape the **pizza dough**!

92

✳✳✳✳✳✳✳✳✳✳✳✳✳✳✳✳✳

Pizza Night Pizza

Everyone has a **favourite pizza topping**. What's yours? This recipe uses **lots of veggies** in different colours. Why not try a new flavour of topping each time you **bake**?

 SERVES 2

 15 prep
15 cook

Ingredients
- 125 millilitres (4 fluid ounces) low-fat Greek yogurt
- 130 grams (4¾ ounces) wholemeal flour, plus extra for dusting
- 4 tablespoons All Veggie Sauce (see page 96)
- 4 button mushrooms (about 30 grams/1 ounce), sliced
- ½ small courgette, cut into semicircles
- ¼ bell pepper, sliced
- 2 pitted black olives, sliced
- 3 tablespoons low-salt pizza mix cheese (such as grated mozzarella and Cheddar)

Cooking tools
- Baking sheet
- Large mixing bowl
- Wooden spoon
- Baking parchment
- Rolling pin

1 Preheat the oven to 240°C (220°C fan/475°F/ Gas 9). Heat a baking sheet for 10 minutes.

2 Make the pizza dough. In a large bowl combine the yogurt and flour into a rough mix with a wooden spoon.

(Recipe continues on the next page)

93

3 Put the flour mixture on the worktop. Knead it to make a smooth ball of dough. Use a little more flour for dusting if needed.

4 Put the dough on a large piece of baking parchment. Roll it out into a circle about the size of a dinner plate and the thickness of a coin.

5 Prick the dough all over with a fork. Carefully lift the baking parchment and pizza base onto the hot baking sheet. Cook for 10 minutes.

7 Return to the oven. Cook for a further 5 minutes or until the cheese is melted and starting to brown.

8 Leave to cool for 5 minutes before slicing up. Count the number of slices you have cut.

6 After 10 minutes, take the pizza base out of the oven. Carefully spoon over the All Veggie Sauce. Top with the veggies and cheese.

Chef's tip

Sprinkle **a little flour** over the worktop if your dough sticks when **kneading**.

SERVES 2

 **10 prep
30 cook**

Ingredients
- 100 grams (3½ ounces) wholemeal spaghetti

For the All Veggie Sauce
- 1 carrot, peeled and grated
- 1 small courgette, grated
- 1 red onion, chopped
- 2 garlic cloves, chopped
- 1 small red bell pepper, diced
- 1 celery stick, roughly chopped
- 2 tablespoons tomato puree
- 1 x 400-gram (14-ounce) can chopped tomatoes
- 1 teaspoon balsamic vinegar
- 3 tablespoons olive oil

For Elmo's face
- 2 slices low-salt, low-fat cheese
- ½ yellow bell pepper
- 6 pitted black olives

Cooking tools
- Large saucepan
- Blender
- Round cookie cutter, 3 centimetres (1¼ inches) diameter

Elmo Spaghetti

Elmo isn't able to come to your dinner table, but making his face using spaghetti and **veggie-packed tomato sauce** is the next best thing! It's **fun to make**, and eat!

1 First, make the All Veggie Sauce. Add all the chopped veggies, the tomato puree, and the canned tomatoes to a large pan. Pour in 200 millilitres (7 fluid ounces) water and the balsamic vinegar.

2 Bring to a simmer. Cover and cook over medium heat for 20 minutes.

3 Remove from the heat and leave to cool for 10 minutes. Meanwhile cook the pasta following the packet instructions.

4 When the sauce has cooled, add the olive oil. Carefully transfer to a blender and blend for 1 minute until the sauce is velvety smooth.

5 Once the pasta is cooked, drain and divide between serving bowls. Top each serving with 3 tablespoons of the sauce. Make a circle shape in the centre.

6 Use the round cookie cutter to cut 2 circles from each slice of cheese for eyes (see Chef's tip, right). Cut two 5-centimetre (2-inch) ovals from a piece of yellow pepper for a nose. Cut 4 slices of olives for pupils.

7 Use the cheese circles and olive slices for eyes. Make Elmo's mouth from pieces of chopped olives.

8 Any remaining sauce can be frozen in portions for up to 3 months. You could use it to make a pizza base (see page 92).

Chef's tip

If you don't have a **cookie cutter**, use a round object, such as a **jar lid**.

★ ★ ★ ★ ★ ★ ★ ★ ★ ★ ★ ★ ★ ★ ★

Speedy Fried Rice

This **sizzling fried rice** combines tasty turkey with lots of veggies. Finish it with a **splash of soy sauce** and **excellent egg**. It will be ready in no time!

 SERVES 2

 5 prep
15 cook

Ingredients
- 1 teaspoon sunflower oil
- 80 grams (3 ounces) lean minced turkey
- 100 grams (3½ ounces) stir-fry veggies, such as broccoli florets, frozen sweetcorn, peas, or grated carrot
- 2 spring onions, sliced
- 1 garlic clove, crushed
- 140 grams (5 ounces) pre-cooked brown rice, available in a pouch
- 1 tablespoon low-salt soy sauce
- 1 egg, lightly beaten

Cooking tools
- Non-stick frying pan or wok
- Wooden spoon

1 Warm a non-stick pan or wok over a high heat. Add the oil. Cook the turkey for about 5 minutes, until starting to brown.

2 Reduce the heat to medium–high. Scatter in all the chopped veggies, spring onions, and garlic. Add the cooked rice and pour over the soy sauce.

3 Keep stir-frying with a wooden spoon for 4–5 minutes. Make sure that everything cooks and the rice is reheated until piping hot.

4 Pour over the beaten egg. Stir the egg through the rice until it is set and cooked. Divide the fried rice between serving bowls.

Helping hand

To **prepare the egg,** crack it into a bowl. Use a fork to break the yolk and **mix it into the white.**

HEALTHY TREATS

★ ★ ★ ★ ★ ★ ★ ★ ★ ★ ★ ★ ★ ★ ★

Rainbow Wands

Once you've **eaten a rainbow** you will always remember the order of the colours: **red**, **orange**, **yellow**, **green**, **blue**, and **purple**! Match the fruit with its colour as you thread them on the skewer.

 SERVES 2

 15 prep

Ingredients
- 6 blueberries
- ½ kiwi, peeled and cut into 4 chunks
- ¼ ripe mango, peeled and cut into 4 chunks
- ½ orange or mandarin, peeled and broken into segments
- 4 strawberries, halved
- 6 raspberries
- 2 tablespoons low-fat Greek yogurt
- ½ teaspoon vanilla extract

Cooking tools
- 2 wooden skewers, sharp ends removed
- Bowl and fork

1 Taking care with the tip, thread each skewer with fruit: 3 blueberries, 2 chunks of kiwi, 2 chunks of mango, 2 orange segments, 1 strawberry half, and 1 raspberry.

2 Mash the remaining raspberries and strawberries in a bowl with a fork.

3 Mix the mashed fruit with the yogurt and vanilla. Serve as a dip for the skewers.

HEALTHY HABITS

Try to eat a colourful **rainbow of fruit** and **veggies** every day!

* * * * * * * * * * * * * * * * * * * *

Bert's Best Crumble

This **crispy topping** uses **Bert's favourite ingredient**, oats, to make it healthy and tasty. **Peaches and raspberries are summer fruits** but you can make a crumble **with any fruit** that's in season.

 SERVES 2

 10 prep
15 cook

Ingredients
- 1 small peach, peeled, stoned, and chopped into chunks
- 10 raspberries
- 2 teaspoons low-fat Greek yogurt, to serve

For the crumble topping
- 1 tablespoon self-raising wholemeal flour
- 3 tablespoons porridge oats
- 1 tablespoon low-fat cream cheese

Cooking tools
- 2 small ovenproof dishes or ramekins
- Mixing bowl
- Baking sheet

1 Preheat the oven to 200°C (180°C fan/400°F/Gas 6). Divide the fruit between the dishes.

2 Add the flour, oats, and cream cheese to a small mixing bowl. Rub together with your fingertips to make a rough crumb.

3 Sprinkle the topping onto the fruit. Place the dishes on a baking sheet. Bake in the oven for 12–15 minutes, until the fruit juices start to bubble and the crumble topping is crisp.

4 Leave to cool a little and serve topped with a dollop of yogurt.

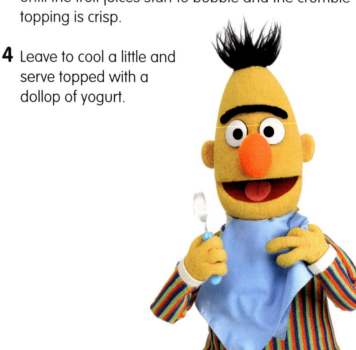

Helping hand

You don't need tools to **make a crumble topping**, just use your fingers to **rub, rub, rub**!

★ ★ ★ ★ ★ ★ ★ ★ ★ ★ ★ ★ ★ ★ ★ ★

"Me Love Cookies" Cookies

These **monstrously delicious** cookies are made for sharing with your friends and family. **Cookie Monster** would probably eat these with anything, but they do taste especially nice with a glass of **milk**.

MAKES 14

15 prep
10 cook

Ingredients
- 150 grams (5½ ounces) self-raising wholemeal flour
- 50 grams (1¾ ounces) soft brown sugar
- 1 teaspoon vanilla extract
- 100 grams (3½ ounces) low-fat cream cheese
- 40 grams (1¼ ounces) dark chocolate chips

Cooking tools
- 2 baking sheets lined with baking parchment
- Food processor
- Mixing bowl
- Fork

1 Preheat the oven to 200°C (180°C fan/400°F/Gas 6). Add the flour, sugar, vanilla, and cream cheese to a food processor. Pulse the mixture until it starts to come together into a soft dough.

2 Turn out into a mixing bowl. Add the chocolate chips. Gently mix together with your hands to form a dough.

3 Scoop out 14 tablespoons of cookie dough. Roll into rough balls between your hands. Place on the baking sheets.

4 Press down each ball of dough with the back of a fork. Bake in the oven for 9–10 minutes. Leave to cool completely before serving.

5 Store in an airtight container for up to 1 week. If you want to bake a smaller batch, any uncooked dough can be frozen for up to 1 month. Defrost before cooking as above.

Chef's tip

Swap out the chocolate chips for **blueberries** to make a **fruity cookie**.

* * * * * * * * * * * * * * * *

Pretty Pink Drink

This healthy drink of **strawberries and spinach** can be mixed up **super quick**. It looks pretty enough for a party but you can have it anytime! **Who will you share it with**?

 SERVES 2

 5 prep

Ingredients
- 5 strawberries, halved
- A handful of baby spinach (about 10 grams/¼ ounce)
- 3 tablespoons low-fat Greek yogurt
- 2 tablespoons low-fat (semi-skimmed) milk

Cooking tools
- Blender
- Paper straw, optional

1 Put 2 strawberry halves to one side. Add all the remaining ingredients to a blender and blend until smooth. Divide between glasses.

2 Cut a slit halfway up each remaining strawberry half. Slot the strawberry over the rim of each glass. Serve with a paper straw for slurping.

Helping hand

If you **want to eat** the strawberry after, **pinch out the leaves** and stalk from the top.

Mango Fro Yo-Yo

This **frozen yogurt** is bursting with **fruity goodness** and tropical flavours. On a hot summer's day, **you can mix this up** in no time for a tasty cool-down while you sit in the shade.

 SERVES 2

 15 prep

Ingredients
- 120 grams (4 ounces) chopped frozen mango
- 3 tablespoons low-fat Greek yogurt
- A handful (about 25 grams/ 1 ounce) of mixed berries, such as blueberries, strawberries, and/or raspberries, halved

Cooking tools
- Blender
- Spatula

1 Take the mango chunks out of the freezer 10 minutes before you make the frozen yogurt.

2 Add the mango and yogurt to a blender and pulse for 20 seconds. Carefully push down the sides of the mixture with a spatula. Give a gentle stir.

3 Keep blending and stirring until you achieve a smooth, thick ice-cream texture.

4 Scoop into bowls. Top with a few chopped berries and eat straight away!

5 Any leftovers can be frozen for up to 1 month. Defrost for 10 minutes to soften before serving.

* * * * * * * * * * * * * *

Super Kiwi-Melon Crush

Watermelon and **kiwi** are food **superheroes**! They are full of vitamins that keep everybody healthy. A few slurps of this cooling slushy and you will feel super, like **Super Grover**, too!

 SERVES 2

 5 prep

Ingredients
- 200 grams (7 ounces) watermelon, peeled, deseeded, and chopped into chunks, plus 2 small wedges to garnish
- 1 ripe kiwi, peeled and roughly chopped
- ½ lime
- A handful of ice

Cooking tools
- Blender
- Paper straw, optional

1 Add the chopped fruit to a blender. Squeeze in some lime juice. Blend until smooth.

2 Add the ice and blend again until broken down into a thick slush.

3 Cut a slit down from the point of each watermelon wedge. Slide onto the rim of each glass.

4 Quickly pour the crush between glasses and serve with a paper straw, if you like to slurp.

Helping hand
Using your **strong muscles**, help to **squeeze** in the lime juice.

Choco-Nana Treat

This yummy combination of **banana and chocolate** has a crispy topping. A **banana gives you lots of energy** for playing a sport or dancing with your friends, like Zoe.

SERVES 2

5 prep
10 chill

Ingredients
- 1 tablespoon low-fat (semi-skimmed) milk
- 2 large squares of dark chocolate (about 20 grams/ ¾ ounce), chopped into small pieces
- 2 small ripe bananas, peeled and whole
- 2 tablespoons puffed rice cereal

Cooking tools
- Heatproof bowl
- Microwave

1 Add the milk to a heatproof bowl. Microwave on low for 10 seconds. Add the chocolate. Stir to melt together into a smooth sauce.

2 Put one whole banana on each plate. Slice into bite-sized pieces, keeping the banana's shape. Drizzle the chocolate sauce over each banana. Scatter with the puffed rice.

3 Chill in the fridge for 10 minutes before serving.

Chef's tip

To drizzle chocolate, **dip a teaspoon** in the melted sauce. Move it in **a zigzag** over the banana.

Magical Hoops

With a **zippity zap** turn juicy slices of apple into **a delicious dessert**. All you need is a dollop of yogurt, a sprinkle of granola, and a cherry on the top. **They're creamy AND crunchy!**

1 Cut 3 slices about 5 millimetres (¼ inch) thick from the middle of each apple.

2 Use an apple corer or small knife to cut the centre core from each apple slice. Keep the slice in one piece.

SERVES 2

10 prep

Ingredients
- 2 small apples, peeled
- 2 tablespoons low-fat Greek yogurt
- 2 tablespoons nut-free granola
- 4 cherries, pitted and chopped into small chunks

Cooking tools
- Apple corer or small knife

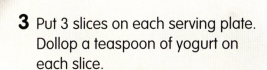

3 Put 3 slices on each serving plate. Dollop a teaspoon of yogurt on each slice.

Chef's tip

Keep any **apple off-cuts** in an airtight container to **enjoy as a snack** later the same day.

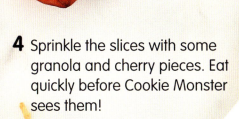

4 Sprinkle the slices with some granola and cherry pieces. Eat quickly before Cookie Monster sees them!

Glossary

Allergy
This is when your body reacts to something, such as a type of food, and it makes you feel unwell. Some people need to take medicine to help them feel better.

Anytime foods
These are healthy foods that you should include in everyday meals, including fruit and vegetables, wholemeal or whole-wheat options for bread or pasta, low-fat dairy, and low-salt alternatives.

Crudités
These are small, crunchy sticks of vegetables, such as peeled cucumber, carrots, or bell peppers, that you can eat as a snack or use for dunking in tasty dips such as hummus.

Dairy
These are foods that are made from milk, such as cheese, yogurt, and ice cream. People who have an allergy to dairy can swap in plant-based options to use in the recipes instead.

Fibre
This is a nutrient found in whole grains, fruits, vegetables, and beans. It is important to include fibre in your meals to keep food moving through your body. It also fills up your tummy so that you don't feel so hungry.

Minerals
Your body needs small amounts of these nutrients to stay healthy and strong. Calcium is a mineral found in foods, especially dairy foods such as yogurt. Calcium helps your teeth and bones to grow strong.

Nutrients
These are important substances in food that your body needs to stay healthy and grow. Vitamins and minerals are nutrients that are found in anytime foods, especially fruit and vegetables.

Omega-3
This is a type of nutrient mainly found in oily fish, such as salmon. It helps keep your body healthy and strong.

Plant-based
These are foods that don't contain meat, eggs, or dairy. There are plant-based milks that are made from oats or soya. You can swap in plant-based options for meat or dairy ingredients in recipes.

Portion
This is the amount of food for one person. A whole dish, such as a pizza or quesadilla, needs to be divided into portions before serving, depending on the number of people.

Side dish

This is an extra amount of food that is served with the main meal. Salads and cooked veggies, such as broccoli, are side dishes.

Sometimes foods

These are special occasion treats, such as cookies, that you can eat once in a while, not every day.

Superfoods

Some foods have lots of nutrients, so they are very healthy. Lots of brightly coloured fruits and veggies, such as tomatoes and broccoli, are superfoods.

Vitamins

These are nutrients that your body needs from food to keep you healthy. Vitamin C is found in many fruits, especially oranges, and helps your body fight off germs.

Wholemeal or whole-wheat

Wheat is a type of whole grain. Whole grains, or foods made from them, contain all the essential parts and naturally occurring nutrients of the entire grain seed. Wholemeal bread or pasta is a healthy choice when cooking.

Index

Cooking Together

Here are just some of the ways that you and the child in your life can explore cooking together. Involving your child in preparing meals can help them establish healthy habits and gain confidence in trying new foods.

- Take a quiet moment to sit and choose a recipe together. Choose "anytime" foods for everyday meals, and turn to the Healthy Treats chapter for "sometimes" foods that can be eaten once in a while.

- Check the cupboards for ingredients. Help your child to either write a shopping list of anything that you need, or for preschool children, you could draw a list.

- At the supermarket, involve your child in adding things to the trolley and selecting ingredients for their chosen recipe.

- In the kitchen, make a safe space for your child to help out at the worktop or kitchen table, so that they can work alongside you and watch. Supervise your child at all times.

- Share the meal together after cooking. Making a family dinner with everyone eating the same meal at the same time is a special feeling.

- As you cook and eat together, encourage your child to describe the colour, taste, and texture of each new food or meal. Which flavours do they like? Can they describe what they don't like and why?

- Have fun tidying up afterwards! Turn water play into a practical skill by helping to wash up any bowls and spoons in lots of bubbles. Wipe the worktop and mop up any spills. This gives your child a special role in the whole cooking experience and will make them feel empowered.

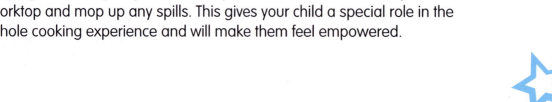

Guide for Grown-Ups

The recipes in this book offer nutritious, fun, and colourful meals to encourage families to establish healthy habits for life. There are a number of ways to encourage the children in your life – and your family – to develop healthy habits when it comes to food.

Balanced diet

It is important to have variety and balance in a child's diet. Help children notice the difference between "anytime" foods, such as fruits and vegetables, that should be eaten every day, and "sometimes" foods, such as cookies, that can be eaten occasionally. Snacks also need to be nutritious and contribute to a balanced diet. You can provide snacks to fill in gaps, such as fruits, vegetables, whole grains, and low-fat dairy products.

New foods

Encourage kids to try new and healthy foods. Excite children by suggesting fun ways to eat new foods and exposing them to language to describe the look and taste. Even if a child doesn't like a new food the first time, remain positive. After a few tries, the child might begin to like a new food. Help the child be proud of themselves for trying something new and keep encouraging them to taste new things.

Healthy lifestyle

Food provides energy for exercise, learning, and play. Encourage children to engage in a variety of fun physical activities, including indoor and outdoor play. Foster the joy of physical activity, and highlight exercise as a positive and important aspect of a healthy lifestyle, alongside healthy eating.

Shopping on a budget

There are many ways to eat well on a budget. Bulk buy basics and choose fruit and vegetables when they are in season and less expensive. Look for low-cost protein sources, such as eggs, canned fish, and dried beans. Make a weekly meal plan that uses ingredients for more than one meal. This helps to minimize waste and will focus your shopping so that you only buy what you need. Try to use up leftover vegetables in other recipes to make them go further, too.